MW01004993

The Wit and Wisdom of

Gracie

The Wit and Wisdom of

Gracie

by Gracie Davis

The Wit and Wisdom of Gracie
An Opinionated Pug's Guide to Life
Copyright 2013 by Patti Davis and Huqua Press

All rights reserved.

ISBN 978-0-9838120-5-0

Library of Congress 2013951069

First published in 2013 by Huqua Press
A division of Magpye Media/Morling Manor Corp.
Los Angeles, California

Illustrations by Yoko Matsuoka
Photography by Chloe Moore
Design by designSimple

No wolf was harmed in the illustration of a pug in synthetic wolf cap.

No part of this book may be reproduced or transmitted in any form by any means
without permission from the author or publisher.

HUQUA PRESS

huquapress.com

Printed in the United States of America.

This book is dedicated to my mother, who faithfully transcribed my thoughts. And to my two feline sisters, Aretha and Skeeter (who is now scampering around in Heaven). Thank you for accepting me as a pack member, and for not stealing my toys.

I am a wolf in pug's clothing.

I realize I look nothing like a wolf — I have a smushed-in nose, tiny ears, a curly tail, and a small compact body. But it is a scientific fact that all dogs are descended from wolves. Appearance isn't everything; it's what's inside that counts. And inside every dog is a wolf.

All of us — wolves and their dog descendants — know how important the pack is. Family is at the center of everything. Your family is there to nurture you, protect you, and remind you how important play is…at least that's how we see it. I can only speak for canines. Families evolve over time —the old make way for the new. The pack goes through changes, but one thing remains the same: it's always held together by loyalty and love.

Of course, I didn't know that families change when I was a tiny puppy snuggling against my mother, nursing beside my three siblings. To the untrained eye, the whole nursing thing must appear awfully chaotic sometimes. We were frequently bumping into each other. Paws got in eyes and tails got in mouths. But there was an order to our chaos. For one thing, it's important to stake out the nipple you like and always go straight for it. I preferred one on my mother's left side — I'm not sure why. These days I like sleeping on the left side of the bed…again, not sure why. But I'm getting ahead of myself. Occasionally when my siblings and I went to nurse, I had to push one of my brothers away and remind him that the upper left quadrant of our mother's belly was mine. Some things are just not negotiable.

We lived in a very lovely house with a tennis court that we got to run around on sometimes. I think the idea was to give us exercise, but to us it was just playtime. The nice woman who held us and cleaned us off and took care of us seemed to be able to tell us apart, which was a mystery to me. I thought we all looked pretty much the same.

She called us all by the same name — Puppy. In fact, everyone in the house called us that. It's kind of a funny word. Say it a lot of times really fast — doesn't it just make you laugh?

So in my innocence, I assumed life would go on like that — all of us together, playing and running around. But I

was about to learn an important lesson: Life always changes. The day came when our mother didn't want to nurse us anymore, and the nice lady gave us little bowls of funny looking food that tasted good once I got over the fact that it wasn't my mother's milk. Then other nice people came and visited us. They would cuddle us and pet us and talk in silly whispers. One woman sat on the floor with me for a long time and rolled toys around for me. She was very impressed with my fetching skills. It was clear to me that she was quite smitten.

The next time she came, she picked me up and held me and I felt from her arms that she wasn't going to let me go, which was fine with me because I really liked her. She kept calling me Gracie — I guessed that was now my name — I didn't have a name of my own before, since we were all just called "Puppy." She took me with her on what felt like a long drive, although I now know it wasn't really that long. But at the time it was a big adventure.

We arrived at a house with many windows that looked out over a canyon. I'd never seen so many trees and so much sky. Wow, the world certainly is big, I thought. Then two small creatures with pointy ears and long tails came striding up to us and made terrible hissing noises — right at me! The woman who I now deduced was my new mother called them Aretha and Skeeter and she said something about our new family. Seriously? Family? They were not happy to see

me at all! I know the pack is everything, but this was looking like a very strange pack.

I quickly figured out that these creatures had to be above me on the evolutionary ladder. I mean, why else would they have such attitude? I made up my mind to submit to whatever they wanted. I don't believe submitting is a sign of weakness. I think it's a sign of wisdom. I want to peacefully coexist with everyone, especially bossy little tiger-things who hiss for no apparent reason. Obviously I now know these creatures are called cats. And I would advise any dog to just accept the fact that cats are superior to everyone else. Give in — it makes life easier. Just think how much more peaceful the world would be if humans gave in a little more — rolled on their backs, exposed their throats. This, of course, is wolf behavior, and is encoded in the genes of all dogs. Pity that humans haven't adopted this technique.

I liked my new home. Wind blew through the eucalyptus trees and the moon shone through the bedroom windows. I slept in silver air with soft cushions underneath me. And my mother would get me up a few times at night and take me out on the balcony to a little strip of grass and tell me to pee. Okay, okay, I'm getting this — peeing is done outside. I'm very smart.

Although it took me a little longer to understand that pooping is also done outside.

Anyway…we all started adjusting to our new life together. I quickly realized that Aretha, the black and white little tiger-thing, ruled the house. Skeeter, who had apparently endured a terrible childhood before she was adopted by our mother, was scared of everything. So Skeeter and I bonded, since we were kind of the underlings. And we both obeyed Aretha. So did my mother. Apparently cats are above humans too.

We found our rhythm as a family. Aretha — Miss Bossy-Pants — pretty much dictated how much time Skeeter and I could spend with each other, but that was okay. I needed to nap a lot, being a puppy, so I didn't want to play all the time. My mother introduced me to other dogs at other nice houses — I was really becoming Miss Social Butterfly.

And I figured out the pooping thing — like I said, I'm smart. I don't poop in the house, ever. I poop in driveways — I'm not sure why.

My life was pretty darn good. I sunbathed, I napped, I snuggled in my mother's lap, I learned how cats play from Skeeter, and I let Aretha be the queen.

Just when it seemed like nothing could ever go wrong, a very sad day came. Skeeter had started drooling a lot and not finishing all her food. The morning my mother was taking her to the vet, she tried to leave me at home. But I barked and whined and basically had a tantrum because I knew Skeeter was really sick. So did Aretha. Animals know things that human beings don't. I fussed so much that she gave in and took me along.

Somehow I knew I would be needed. Like I said, the pack is everything, and my instinct told me that sadness was right around the corner. You have to stick by your family at times like these.

The vet showed my mother a huge tumor under Skeeter's tongue. She said it was cancer and it was incurable. Skeeter was in pain and was suffering. She wouldn't be able to eat. My mother started crying and said she didn't want her to suffer any longer than she had. She felt awful that Skeeter had suffered at all. This was why I'd insisted on coming. I got to touch noses with my cat sister and say goodbye just before she slipped away. We left with an empty cat carrier and my mother sobbed the whole way home. Aretha met us at the door and I knew she wasn't surprised. Cats are just as intuitive as dogs. They are, after all, descended from tigers.

Miss Bossy-Pants slept beside me on the bed that night and didn't even try to push me around. Skeeter was a very skittish creature — that's how she got her name — she was always skeeting away. She was definitely a project. But we all missed her. My mother was sad for days and days and there was nothing that Aretha or I could do except comfort her.

It was another big life lesson for me: sometimes you have to say goodbye to the ones you love, and it always seems too soon.

*I got to touch noses
with my cat sister and
say goodbye just before
she slipped away.*

When I was about a year old, the three of us moved out of the canyon and closer to the ocean. Now my mother walks me along wide sidewalks beneath tall trees, and on days when the wind is strong we can smell the sea. We have a big green lawn that looks like a meadow to me, given the fact that I'm rather small. Aretha lounges in the sun and watches birds who know that she's a bit too old to go after them. One day I saw a bird almost hop on top of her. Boy was that bird brave!

Buddha came along with us — not in person, of course, but the statue that sat outside at our hillside home. Now he sits beneath a huge shade tree and I still get to commune with him. I've learned that it's healthy to have a strong spiritual practice, so I make a point of nuzzling up to Buddha.

Here's another thing I've learned: neighborhoods are important. You need to walk out your door, down the sidewalk, and know that you'll run into friends and share your walks with them. I can't imagine what life would be if I couldn't walk with my friends.

I'm all about discovery. I am constantly open to new things and I believe strongly that this is vital to living a productive and ever-evolving life. For the benefit of humans, who like to have their information organized, I will address my discoveries in sections:

1

There is More Than One Way to Hold a Pug

Holding a pug is an art form. Individuality must be taken into account, and respected. I have a pug friend named Nugget, who only wants to be held facing a human with her front legs draped over the person's shoulders. Personally, I would find that uncomfortable. I made it very clear to my mother right from the get-go how I wanted to be held — sideways, with one of her arms beneath my front legs and (this is very important) the other arm between my back legs. Not to be crude, but I don't like my hoo-hoo to dangle. The first time I went to a grooming appointment, my mother had to specify this to the groomer who now has it memorized.

Before she takes me in back for my spa treatment, she carries me in the manner I have deemed acceptable. It's just one other thing that is not negotiable.

2

They Paved Paradise,
But I Can Still Smell It

When we moved to our new house and I began to explore the cement patio in back, I had a revelation. Things are buried under cement! This is also true for bricks, flagstones, and pretty much any stone surface that has been laid down over Mother Earth. The earth contains millions of stories. Just because you put cement and stone on top, it doesn't mean those stories evaporate. They're still there, each with a distinct scent that I, Gracie, descendant of wolves, can detect.

When I first made this amazing discovery, I tried desperately to tell my mother about it by pawing at the cement, running around in circles and making little yipping sounds. Look, look, I was saying! There is something beneath this surface! Layers of earth and history — life, death, memories and… well, I don't really know what else…just stuff!

She looked at me calmly and said, "Did you just become a bloodhound?"

Oh, for Pete's Sake, what a ridiculous thing to say. I might not be a bloodhound, but I can detect stuff that's buried. A dog's sense of smell is thousands of times greater than humans — that's why they use us for important detective work. Okay, they might not use pugs, but I think that's just because we're small. Shepherds always get the important jobs.

When my mother and I go plant shopping, I tug on the leash, put my nose to the ground and do my best to announce to everyone at the nursery that I am on the trail of long-buried artifacts. People laugh and say, "Oh that's so cute!"

IT IS NOT CUTE! I am doing important work, I don't know why it isn't more appreciated. What really puzzles me is that none of my dog friends are the least bit interested in this. They just watch me and then go roll in the grass or something. Do they not care that Homo Sapiens have paved over vast stretches of history? Or maybe it's that my sense of smell is superior to that of other dogs. Maybe my friends just can't pick up on the same scents I can. I don't have any bloodhound friends — presumably a bloodhound would be right there with me. If anyone knows a bloodhound, could you please put him in touch with me? I'm easy to find — I have my own Facebook page.

3

Little Red Corvette

I might have a few less objections if the automotive industry had stopped at little red Corvettes, or Corvettes of any color. But no! They clearly went hog-wild with automobiles of all sizes.

I do not understand for the life of me how humans let cars and trucks just rumble right past them on the street as if this is not a cause for alarm. Why don't these two-legged creatures yell and lunge at such an intrusion? (Yelling of course being the human equivalent of barking.) I thought my mother would be proud of me for taking a stand against all the big noisy vehicles. But no! She even took me to dog classes so I would learn to not do that. That didn't work very well. I did learn some things — I learned to sit, stay, come, and heel. I learned to walk in tight little circles right beside her legs, which seems totally senseless to me. When are you going to need that in the real world? It's like teaching a dog Algebra. What possible use would there be for that? Anyway, I learned all the obedience stuff and the instructor praised me, and everyone liked me. But I still barked at cars.

One day when we were on our afternoon walk my mother yanked on the leash and said No! just as I was starting to lunge at a FedEx truck. Then she said, in a rather exasperated tone, "I don't understand this car thing! Are you from another planet?"

Well, I'm glad you asked, I thought. Because I believe I am. I am from Planet Pug, and on my planet we do not tolerate big vehicles with engines and wheels. We bark at them, we scare them away, and it always works! And no one makes us stop. Because on Planet Pug the pugs get to do whatever they want whenever they want. So there!

Of course she didn't really hear a word I was saying — it just sounded like snorts and yips to her. Humans never have been able to crack the code of dog-speak. (They're a little unevolved that way.)

So she began to carry a small spray bottle with her when we walked and it was filled with water. Whenever I barked at a vehicle she sprayed me! Sometimes right in the butt! This is absolutely unacceptable!

"Call PETA!" I cried to passersby. "Notify the Humane Society!"

But of course they didn't know what I was saying either. Oh, these lowly humans, whatever are we to do with them?

I am from Planet Pug, and on my planet we do not tolerate big vehicles with engines and wheels.

AND THEN… as if the water thing wasn't enough, my mother made me sit at every intersection and not set a paw over the curb until she said I could. Well, I know this game. She's trying to be Alpha Dog. Fine, fine — I'll let you be Alpha on our walks but you will never have the wisdom and knowledge of a dog, sister. You need me for that.

By the way, my favorite day of the week is Tuesday. That's trash truck day. They might not admit it, but the men driving those big green trucks are shaking with fear when see the wrath of Gracie on the sidewalk right next to them. My mother may have stopped me from barking at other vehicles, but trash trucks are in a league of their own, and I will not be silenced.

Another thing about wheels: I'm flummoxed by kids zipping past on little pieces of wood that have wheels on the bottom that make a terrible clattering sound as they're careening down the street. The kids are standing on these contraptions with nothing to hold onto. The whole thing looks very precarious. Why are they doing this? They have feet for God's sake — and feet were made for walking.

And as if taking over the streets wasn't enough, there are engines in the sky! One day I was lounging in the sun, feeling all warm and relaxed, when I heard the sound of an engine that seemed to be high above me. At first I thought I was dreaming. But then I sat up and looked above the tree-tops. There, miles and miles away, in the blue waves of sky, was some kind of silver vehicle that clearly had an engine.

So I barked at it — of course. My mother came outside and said in a soothing tone of voice, "It's just a plane, Gracie."

A plane? What's a plane? And why is that supposed to make me feel better? It has an engine and it's in the sky! You people put engines everywhere, it's just not rational. I can accept birds in the sky — although I bark at them too sometimes — but big metal things with engines? Who comes up with these hair-brained ideas?

Of course, I have to be honest and admit that I do like riding in my mother's car. I have a car seat, which gives me a view, and I usually like where she takes me…unless it's to the vet's office, and then I don't. Maybe there should only be cars for dog passengers. That would do a lot to ease the traffic situation. If this were Planet Pug, we'd just ban the other vehicles.

4

Rainy Days and Mondays Always Get Me Down

I don't really mean Mondays — I just heard that song on the radio one day when I was in the car with my mother. She started singing along to it. Very embarrassing. Anyway, I have no problem with Mondays. I do, however, have a problem with rainy days. And with baths. Probably no one would ever write a song saying *Rainy days and baths always get me down.* That would be silly.

Anyway…I have a problem with both.

Let me first address the days when water falls from the sky. Why can't it just rain at night? I don't mind the sound of rain on the roof — it's soothing and I'm a romantic at heart. Besides, I'm inside so I don't really mind that water is falling from the sky. But it should stop raining at dawn. Period.

Well, apparently God has other ideas because there are days when it just rains and rains and rains. I have a pink raincoat with a hood on it, and while I know I look fetching in it, it doesn't keep me completely dry. My mother walks with an umbrella over us, but that isn't always foolproof either. I return from these outings with my legs and paws wet, oftentimes my ears, since the hood falls back when I'm walking, and there have actually been occasions when the top of my head got rained upon! Might I suggest that someone construct a small wheeled device (since humans love wheels so much) that will accommodate a dog of my size on rainy days and can just be pulled along by the accompanying human?

Sort of like a Popemobile. Only it would be a Pugmobile. Of course this doesn't really address the fact that walking means we are expected to poop and pee, and one can't exactly do that in the vehicle one is riding in. We would have to emerge from said vehicle for those necessities. But the rest of the time we would be able to stay dry. It seems a very civilized mode of transportation. I figure if it's good enough for the Pope, it's good enough for a pug.

Might I suggest that someone construct a small wheeled device that will accommodate a dog of my size on rainy days...?

Now…baths. I realize cleanliness is next to Godliness, but that doesn't mean I enjoy being immersed in water, even warm water. As I mentioned previously, my mother takes me to a wonderful groomer. She sings to me and gives me an acupressure massage, as well as a blueberry facial. I love her! And I of course love my mother, who sometimes, between grooming appointments, bathes me in the tub. I don't blame my mother for not knowing acupressure, or for being completely ignorant when it comes to blueberry facials. She's a writer, not a groomer — I get that.

But do I have to be clean all the time? What's wrong with having the scent of soil and grass on me? As well as the occasional I-don't-know-what-this-is-but-it's-a-deliciously-funky mystery scent? I haven't researched this extensively, but I am pretty sure wolves don't get baths.

Anyway, my mother seems unrelenting on the whole cleanliness thing. There is a silver lining though: Whenever I get wet, I get dried off with a big fluffy towel, and then my favorite — the blow-dryer! I first discovered the blow-dryer when I was just a wee puppy and my mother got out of the shower with wet hair, removed from a drawer this amazing contraption that blows warm air! I ran into the bathroom, nuzzled against her legs and yipped a few times. She understood what I wanted and from then on, whenever she dries her hair, she has to share the dryer with me, whether I'm wet or not.

Of course, when I am wet I get the blow-dryer all to myself, which is the best, because deep inside, I'm really rather selfish.

Sometimes she takes me to visit the salon where she gets her hair trimmed, and I get to sit in one of those big swivel chairs while the hairdresser blow-dries me. Everyone in the salon giggles and has such fun with this, which is fine, although I don't see what the big deal is. It's a wonderful experience being flooded with warm air. Doesn't everyone like it?

Apparently not. I've learned there are dogs who find the blow-dryer frightening. Well, this is just sad. They must have endured some terrible experience in their formative years that left them with a completely irrational fear. Childhood traumas are very difficult to recover from.

Speaking of cleanliness, my mother is a little OCD about teeth. Her own and mine. The one thing I'm grateful for is that she doesn't try to floss my teeth, which she does to her own numerous times a day.

What she does do to me is take me in every six months for a non-anesthesia teeth cleaning. In case you don't know what this entails, I am wrapped in swaddling clothes and laid in a woman's lap, who then proceeds to pick and scrape at my teeth. The wrapping isn't actually swaddling clothes, it's a big towel. But I do either resemble Baby Jesus or a burrito, depending on your frame of reference.

Anyway, I find it very annoying, although I have to say my mouth feels quite clean and shiny after it's all done. So I guess the annoyance of the whole thing is worth it. I have a pug friend named Lola who had to have some teeth removed! OMG, I couldn't even listen to that conversation, it made me so queasy!

Surfing USA

4

Okay, to be clear — my mother has not made me surf. I heard that song on the radio, too. Thankfully, she didn't sing along to that one. There isn't, to my knowledge, a song called Swimming USA.

And she did decide that swimming was an appropriate activity for me, which is about as ridiculous as it gets. What about in winter? Will I be expected to take up ice-skating? Skiing?

The swimming idea came about because we were at a friend's house one warm summer day and I fell into the pool. I was scooped out in about three seconds, although I wasn't in trouble, I was paddling, as any dog knows how to do. We do have instincts, you know. Anyway, my mother really over-reacted, in my opinion.

"We have to teach you where the steps are!" she cried.

Well, I'm sure I would have found them — you all dove in and took me out of the pool in a New York minute! (I don't actually know what a New York minute is, I've just heard it said. Is it different from a regular minute?)

She then carried me into the shallow end of the pool, aimed me toward the steps and watched protectively as I paddled toward them. Fine, I know where they are now — can we get out? No! I had to do it a few more times. In the process, she noticed a rather inconvenient body issue particular to pugs and a few other breeds — our butts start sinking as we paddle. We are not built for water sports.

As you might expect, she had a solution for this; she bought me a bright yellow floatie and when it arrived, into the pool we went again, aiming for the steps. I must say, even though I'm not partial to water, it was kind of fun being so buoyant. And it was a hot day, so I got cooled off as well.

I had to apologize to some of my other canine friends because their humans then decided this was a good idea. It really isn't ...unless you're a Labrador Retriever and then it probably is.

Recently I was reunited with my brother. His name is Quincy, and his mother contacted my mother...well, of course that led to a play date, and when I saw that Quincy had a pool at his house, I knew what was coming.

Sure enough, my mother took me to buy a floatie for Quincy so we could swim together. "Won't he love this?"

44

she gushed, as she made me try it on for size (we are almost exactly the same size.) Probably not, I thought. He might think you're off your rocker.

He actually looked quite fetching in his green floatie, and except for swimming into the side of the pool once, he did well for his first aquatic adventure. After a few tries, he knew to just follow me to the steps and climb out. I have to brag here and say that his mother commented on my superior form. I do have a very graceful stroke. It's nice when people notice such things.

I Want My MTV

5

Not really. Unless there are animals on it. I want Animal Planet, the Discovery Channel, and many re-runs of the Nasonex commercial with the fake buzzing bees. I get very excited when I see four-legged creatures behind that glass screen where they can't respond to me as I bark and do wheelies in front of them. I'm not sure why I like the fake talking bees so much, I just do.

One evening my mother was watching a show about gorillas and apes. I was going bonkers! When in real life would I get a chance to bark at a silver-backed gorilla with no consequences? It was exhilarating! I did not appreciate it when my mother brought over the spray bottle and sprayed water at me because she said she wanted to watch the show. I'm watching it too, I thought, I just happen to have things to say about it.

On another occasion, she watched a show with many dogs on it and some dude who calls himself a "Whisperer." What in the world does that mean? He isn't whispering, I can hear him just fine. This time, she wanted me to sit beside her and learn from this whisperer person (who was not whispering at all) because he was getting the dogs to do what he said and be obedient. At that point, I stopped having fun.

Rise up! I thought helplessly, wishing the dogs could hear me through the glass screen. Don't give up your wild ways! We are wolves, remember? Assert yourselves! Don't take that lying down!

Well, my psychic brainwaves didn't penetrate the glass screen. I watched dejectedly as they lay down. And sat. And walked right in line with their owners. I knew what was coming.

My line in the sand when we went to obedience classes was lying down. I simply refused. I don't know why. I'm quite fond of lying down; I just want to do it on my own terms. But now my mother was determined that she would go all alpha on me and get me to lie down when she wanted me to. We had a bit of a stand-off, and I have to admit I was getting bored with the whole thing. So I did it. She was so elated she went and got me a treat, which sort of made the whole ordeal worthwhile.

Other than animals on television, I've taken a liking to several humans. I love Bruce Springsteen…there's just something about him. I'm also partial to Jon Stewart and Anderson Cooper. When my mother goes out in the evening, she leaves CNN on for me, so I can watch Anderson. I find his voice very soothing. Does anyone know if he has a dog? Maybe we could schedule a play date.

One evening she left a different channel on, and I found myself riveted by someone named Dr. Drew and a bunch of humans who were, quite frankly, a mess. When my mother returned, I didn't budge or greet her because, as I said, I was riveted.

"What are you watching?" she asked, sitting down beside me.

I glanced at her, then glanced back at the television. Isn't it obvious? I thought.

"Celebrity Rehab? You're watching Celebrity Rehab?"

Yes, and you're interrupting me. This Dr. Drew person is trying very hard to get through to that drooling woman who is paying absolutely no attention to him. I certainly hope she doesn't have a dog.

One thing I've learned is that people can find a lot of ways to mess up their lives. They should think more like dogs. We're very reasonable. Dogs only go off the deep end if humans push us off it, which is terribly sad and should be prosecuted to the full extent of the law.

"Celebrity Rehab?
You're watching
Celebrity Rehab?"

Yes, and you're
interrupting me.

Uptown Girl

Nothing makes a girl feel better than strutting down the sidewalk knowing that she seriously rocks. We live near a fashionable street that, without doubt, sees its share of strutting on a daily basis. But when my mother takes me shopping, I can prance with the best of them. Better than most, I think. I mean, just look at my booty. People stop in their tracks, stare in admiration; they ask my name and then they ask to pet me. They coo and fuss and tell my mother how adorable I am. Like, duh — we know that.

Anyway, I have my favorite stores along this street. Shabby Chic is my absolute favorite! And they love me in there. I'm sort of the product tester. I jump on one sofa, then another…then I choose which one I like best. Once I choose, I pose as if I'm being photographed for a store ad,

which I think I should be. Then I look at my mother with pleading eyes…Please, can't we buy this sofa and take it home? Please? Please?

The answer is always the same: "Sorry, honey, but it's very expensive. We can't afford it."

But I'm here boosting business by showing how luscious the furniture is! I'm a great advertisement for Shabby Chic — look how perfectly I blend with this style! Shouldn't that be worth something?

Apparently not. We've been through this a million times and the answer is always the same. I can be patient, though. As well as persistent. I am not giving up on the sofa of my dreams. That sofa is in my future, I just know it. And maybe I'll even let my mother sit on it too.

Our other stops include the beauty salon, which I mentioned before — we zip in so I can get a quick blow dry. A few doors down is a jewelry store where my largest friend — a Great Dane named Maggie — hangs out two days a week. Her mother works there and Maggie has become the store mascot. They even put her picture on the door with emeralds around her neck! So I have to go in and greet Maggie with a friendly, What's up?

What's usually up with her is: she's playing with her VERY LARGE monkey toy, and her VERY LARGE rawhide chew-thing. She doesn't mind if I get near monkey, but she got mad at me once when I sniffed at her rawhide firelog. For God's sake, did she think I was going to walk off with it? It's nearly as big as I am. Anyway, we worked things out, as dogs tend to do. At the risk of being indelicate, the one problem with having such a tall friend is, it's impossible to sniff her butt. I mean, I can't get above her knees! But other than that, I love her very much.

My mother and I occasionally have lunch along the street, sitting at an outside cafe where waiters bring me bowls of water. It's very civilized. Of course, the temptation to bark at passing cars is tremendous, and there have been times when I seriously back-slid, got into a barking frenzy, and my mother had to hold me in her lap to calm me down and keep me quiet. I think I ruined her lunch, as it's hard to eat with a pug in your lap. But she didn't complain; she just soldiered on. That's the way it is with us — we stick together through the peaks and valleys. Love conquers all…even the overwhelming temptation of a UPS truck rumbling past.

Dream, Dream, Dream

In my dreams I am bounding across wide green fields with blue mountains in the distance and billowy white clouds floating in the skies above me. I'm chasing rabbits. I have no idea why. They're running, so I'm running.

But the point is, in my dreams, the earth has a lot more room on it. There are miles of grassy land, there are forests and lakes (not that I go in the lakes, but I appreciate them) and rocky cliffs with caves and dens for animals who need shelter from storms. In my dreams, there are no streets, and — I have to say — no cars. I bark at bunnies instead of buses.

It seems so real, those wide open miles and bright blue skies. Often when I wake up, my dreams don't fade. I walk along sidewalks, but I can still see fields with waving grasses. Also in my dreams, I can run like some of the animals I've

seen on the Discovery Channel — gazelles and cheetahs. In real life, I'm able to pick up speed with my little legs when I spot a friend of mine up ahead. Sometimes my mother complains because she's wearing flip-flops and I'm making her run in the wrong shoes. But I'm never as fast as I am in my dreams.

I think dreams are important. They show us what we could do if we just lived in our imaginations. They show us what we're really made of. I, of course, am made of wolf blood. Sometimes I've seen Aretha's paws moving when she's sleeping. I wonder if in her dreams she's a tiger in the Serengeti. I've tried to ask her but she just flicks her tail at me and walks away. She has such attitude!

Fit and Fabulous

8

Other than cleanliness and dental hygiene, my mother is also very strict about diet and fitness. I would eat anything anytime. Most pugs would. I would certainly accept the treats that are offered in almost every business we frequent, even the bank. But my mother always says, "No thank you." I get a tiny bit of cut-up chicken in the morning, because Aretha does, and then I have to wait until sunset for my meal. I must say, that end-of-day feeding time is the best hour of the day.

These dietary restrictions, as well as my regular walks, have kept me in fabulous shape. Everyone comments on my figure. So I'm grateful to my mother for that. And I'm particularly grateful that she doesn't make me lift weights and run for miles like she does. It's important to recognize that not everyone has to do the same exercise.

When I'm Sixty-Four

9

I know, when I'm sixty-four (in dog years of course) that my mother will be patient and tender with me, because she is with Aretha these days. Aretha is seventeen, which is fairly old for a cat. She sleeps a lot now — all through the day mostly. Then at night she wakes up sometimes and meows in a very mournful way. My mother calls out to her and she eventually jumps on the bed, which seems to calm her down.

She often seems a bit confused. She'll meow at a closet door like she wants to go in there, but when my mother opens it, Aretha looks up at her like she doesn't understand. My mother said she probably has kitty Alzheimer's. I'm not exactly sure what that is, but it doesn't sound good.

Lately she isn't interested in her food. She'll eat it if my mother puts handfuls down in front of her where she's lying, but if she gets up on the table where her dish is, she looks confused and climbs back down. My mother has discovered that she'll eat a bit of salmon sashimi, but only if she can eat it under the bed. Even then she looks confused, but if we leave her alone, she'll usually finish her fish.

My mother tries not to show that she's sad, but I know she is. I'm sad too. Even though Aretha is Miss Bossy-Pants, she's a member of my pack. I've accepted her quirks, and I've let her be the queen because that's just what you have to do sometimes when you care about someone.

Whenever Aretha has to go to the vet, I go too. My mother doesn't even try to leave me at home. We're a family, and we have an elderly family member who needs all the care we can give her. That said, if she doesn't eat the hand-fuls of cat food that are put down in front of her, I will try to get them. (My mother is generally faster than I am and intercepts my efforts, but I do try.)

10

Imagine

Imagine what the world would be like if everyone thought like me. If humans believed in submission as an appropriate gesture when first meeting a stranger and practiced it as the art form it is. The planet would be a very peaceful place. Of course, you'd have to be careful when walking along sidewalks because there would probably be many people lying down on their backs and exposing their jugulars to strangers who are then obligated to spend some time sniffing them. But that would slow everyone down, which would be very beneficial as well…in my opinion, anyway.

Imagine what the world would sound like with less engines. You'd be able to hear other things, like crickets chirping and birds singing; cats meowing and dogs snoring. The skies would be wide and endless, with the soft sound of wind pushing clouds along and the cries of hawks echoing across blue miles. And of course I would not have to wake up from my naps to bark at those pesky airplanes that have no business rumbling along up there in the first place. I think the world used to be like that — a long time ago. I'm not sure how I know that, it's just a thought that came to me.

Imagine if every family was like a wolf family — bonded together with loyalty and unwavering love. If humans understood that the pack is everything, there would never be any sad children or lonely people who then get angry and try to hurt others just because they're hurt. Wolves and all their descendants (of which I am one, as I have made abundantly clear) are very wise. We understand what's most important in life: love.

Imagine if everyone dreamed the way I do — if in dreamland they raced across green meadows and up gentle hillsides, never getting tired, never stumbling or falling. My mother has bad dreams sometimes and it makes me sad because I can't do anything except snuggle up against her to try and make her feel better. I wish I could pull her into my dreams — she'd have so much fun. I don't know if a study has ever been done on this, but I think it's possible that humans are the only species that experience bad dreams.

Imagine if everyone knew how important it is to care for loved ones when they get older and develop some quirks (like wanting to eat off the floor instead of their dishes and curling up in baskets inside the closet.) My sister Aretha gets a little slower each day now, and my mother has to follow her around with handfuls of food, hoping she'll eat some of it. It takes up a lot of time, but that's what you do with the ones you love — you put other things on hold and spend time trying to make them comfortable.

Life really is very short. I learned that when Skeeter died and it made me appreciate every day. Even rainy days when I have to go out in my pink raincoat and I still get raindrops on my face and paws. Behind every rainy day is a blow-dryer. Behind every bath is a soft towel…and a blow-dryer. Behind every sad day, and every bad dream, is something that will make you laugh. I'm very good at making humans laugh — everyone says so. I think that's probably why God made pugs — He knew the world needed more laughter.

Fin

Gracie Davis and her pug swim team were featured in Town and Country *magazine. As team captain, it was her job to keep the other pugs in line, which is difficult in water. This inspired her mother to write about the team and, of course, Gracie's aquatic prowess. Not to be outdone, Gracie decided to embark on her own writing career. This is her first book. She followed the basic rule of writing: write what you know.*